Your Storied Year:

A Journal

Katie Proctor

Copyright 2021 Katie Proctor

Permissions at www.FawkesPress.com

ISBN 978-1-945419-85-0

Dear readers (and writers!),

In My Storied Year, Dragon Stewart learns how powerful words and stories can be. He also learns that even though he is only a seventh grader and has trouble learning sometimes, that he is truly, at his core, a writer. And so are you. My hope in creating Your Storied Year is that you will use it to tell your stories. I hope that you will use it to pay attention to the world around you, your place in it, what's happening around you, and that you will know, too, that your story matters. However your story unfolds-all its joys and all its sorrows-it matters.

These pages can be just for you, a place to record your secrets and thoughts, or it can be shared with whoever you trust with your story. Brain scientists tell us that writing can be an important tool in processing anything that happens to us, big or small. In recounting memorable events, we are able to learn from mistakes, find the good in hard times, and we emerge stronger and better able to face whatever comes next. And, you never know who could benefit from hearing a story like yours.

If you, like Dragon, have some hard things in your life, please know that you are not alone. I hope you have a Denzel or a Mrs. Parkman or a Mr. Mark out there, cheering you on. If not, keep looking, because there are always helpers. And in the times when you do not find yourself in the midst of a struggle, my challenge to you is find ways to be the helper for someone else. You can make such a difference.

Much love and inspiration to you,

Katie Proctor

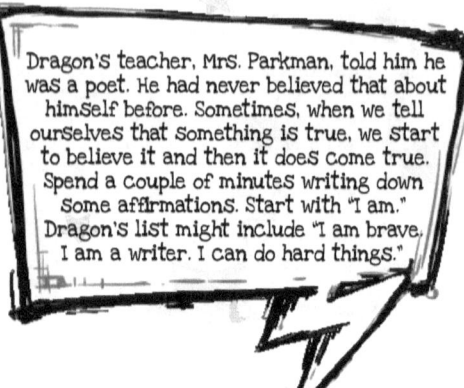

Dragon's teacher, Mrs. Parkman, told him he was a poet. He had never believed that about himself before. Sometimes, when we tell ourselves that something is true, we start to believe it and then it does come true. Spend a couple of minutes writing down some affirmations. Start with "I am." Dragon's list might include "I am brave. I am a writer. I can do hard things."

Choose one of your memories to write about. You can write it just like you remember it, or exaggerate it a little to make it fictional.

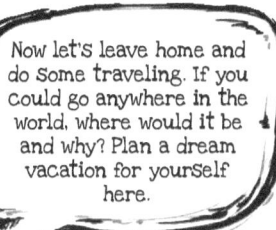

Now let's leave home and do some traveling. If you could go anywhere in the world, where would it be and why? Plan a dream vacation for yourself here.

> Dragon has an unusual name. What's your name? Do you like your name? What does it make you think of? Ask a family member where your name came from and how they decided on that name for you. Do you think your name fits you?

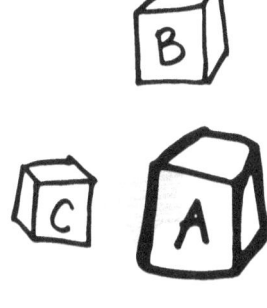

When I read non-fiction, I choose books about:

....
....
....

Books I've loved:

....
....
....
....
....

Books that weren't for me:

....
....
....
....
....

Books I want to read soon:

....
....
....
....
....

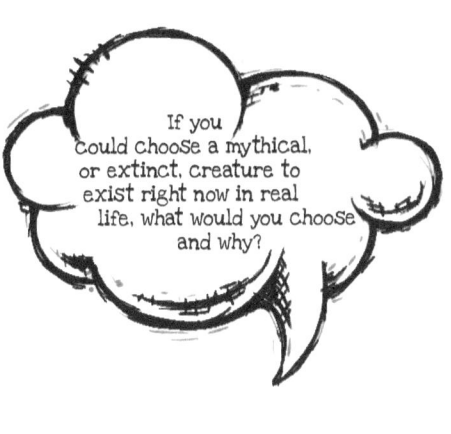

If you could choose a mythical, or extinct, creature to exist right now in real life, what would you choose and why?

Think about your favorite food. What does your perfect food day look like? What would you pick for breakfast, lunch, dinner, and snack?

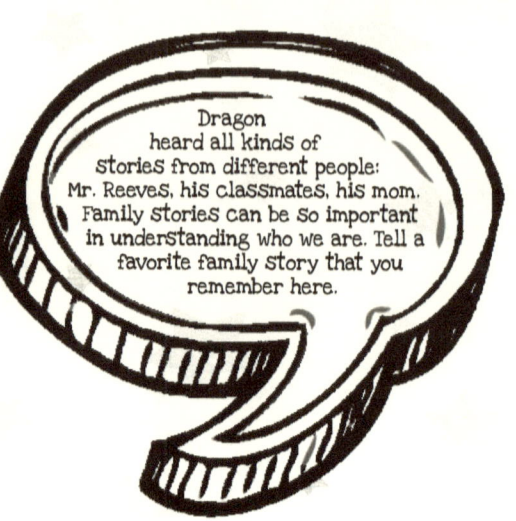

Dragon heard all kinds of stories from different people: Mr. Reeves, his classmates, his mom. Family stories can be so important in understanding who we are. Tell a favorite family story that you remember here.

Now, ask a family member to tell you a favorite story and record it here.

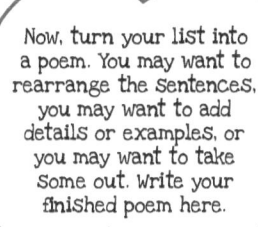

Now, turn your list into a poem. You may want to rearrange the sentences, you may want to add details or examples, or you may want to take some out. Write your finished poem here.

> Dragon has an amazing friend in Denzel. Think about one of your friends. What makes them great? How do you take care of each other?

Dragon also has some great adults in his life: Mrs. Parkman, Ms. Luna, Mr. Mark. Who is a teacher or adult that you trust? What do they do that makes you feel safe?

Dragon has some big feelings in My Storied Year, and he writes about what it feels like when he gets mad or frustrated. Brainstorm what it looks like when you feel a certain way.

Feeling	What does it look like? What does your body do? What do you see/hear/smell when you feel that way?
Anger	
Sadness	
Happiness	

Feeling	What does it look like? What does your body do? What do you see/hear/smell when you feel that way?
Disgust	
Fear	
Embarrassment	
Frustration	

Choose one of the feelings from the page before and write about a time where you had some big feelings like Dragon. What caused you to feel that way? If you needed to, how did you calm yourself down?

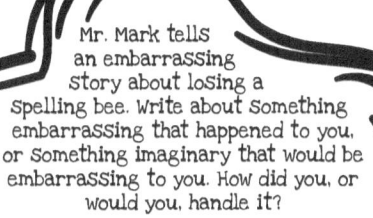

Mr. Mark tells an embarrassing story about losing a spelling bee. Write about something embarrassing that happened to you, or something imaginary that would be embarrassing to you. How did you, or would you, handle it?

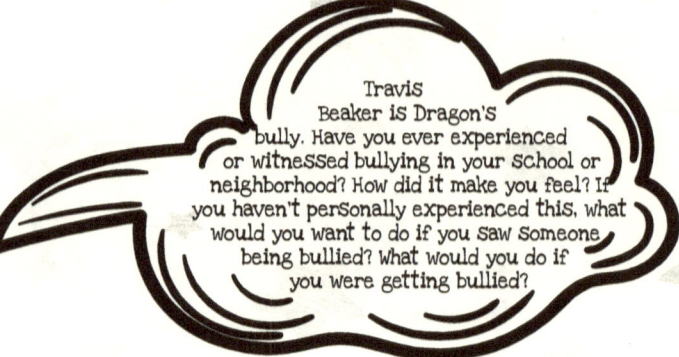

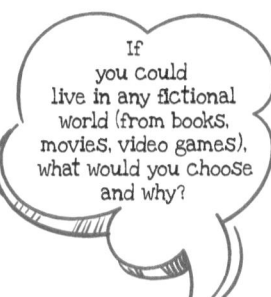

If you could live in any fictional world (from books, movies, video games), what would you choose and why?

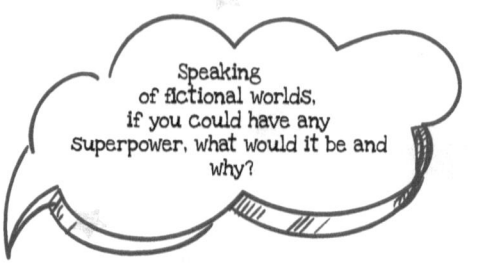

Now write an imaginary story about yourself in that fictional world using your superpower for good.

> Dragon's teachers talk a lot about making mistakes and how we can learn from them. Think about a mistake you made. What did it help you learn? Or realize? And how did you change afterward?

> At Dragon's Christmas party, Denzel gives him a photograph of the two of them and Maya because he knew Dragon wouldn't have a family photo. Think of a time when someone has done something kind and unexpected for you. Write about it.

Make a list of small kindnesses that you could do for your friends, family, or even strangers.

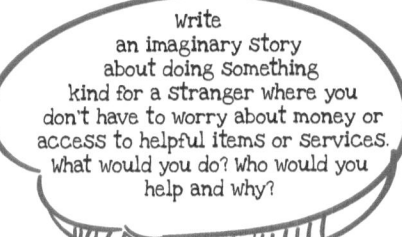

Write an imaginary story about doing something kind for a stranger where you don't have to worry about money or access to helpful items or services. What would you do? Who would you help and why?

Thank you for writing with us! For more reads and writes, please join us at

www.FawkesPress.com/newsletter

If you would like to share your work, have an adult upload a picture and tag us on Instagram @katieproctorwritesandreads and @fawkespress You may also have an adult e-mail a picture to katieproctorwrites@gmail.com We'd love to see your work because YOUR STORY MATTERS!

www.ingramcontent.com/pod-product-compliance
Lightning Source LLC
Chambersburg PA
CBHW030141100526
44592CB00011B/1001